Lessons Learned in Project Management:
140 Tips in 140 Words or Less

John A. Estrella, PhD, PMP

**Lessons Learned in Project Management:
140 Tips in 140 Words or Less**

John A. Estrella, PhD, PMP

ISBN-13: 978-1456357580
ISBN-10: 1456357581

Agilitek Corporation
213-21 Main Street North
Markham, Ontario L3P 1X3
Canada

Phone: (905) 201-3085
Fax: (905) 201-3086
Web: agilitek.com

Preface

About a year ago, I woke up at 4:30 A.M. and could not get back to sleep because a Twitter-inspired book concept kept swirling around in my head. Twitter, as you may know, is a social networking and microblogging service that allows its users to send text messages (tweets) of 140 characters or fewer. The popularity of Twitter provides a clue that brevity is an increasingly preferred characteristic of information. Based on the Twitter concept, I reasoned that if experienced project managers could come up with 140 tips, each in 140 words or less, that would constitute a concise body of knowledge useful for all project managers.

That day, I sent e-mails to my friends, colleagues, Twitter followers, Facebook friends, and LinkedIn connections, asking them each to contribute one tip to be included in this book. Within hours, practical project management tips started coming in. I received tips from project managers in Canada, the United States, South Africa, Poland, the United Kingdom, Argentina, the Cayman Islands, Australia, Brazil, India and other countries.

In about eight months, I was able to compile 64 tips—76 tips short of my target. Along the same timeline, I have been writing project management tips of 140 words or less on my blog at *http://blog.johnestrella.com*. Between the 64 tips that I received and my own tips, I had more than enough to put together this book. (My tips are those that are unsigned, the ones that appear at the end of the book.) I could have finished the book then, but I was too busy at work. It was four months later when I found the time to finalize the book.

To all of my friends, colleagues, Twitter followers, Facebook friends, and LinkedIn connections who helped write this book, thank you very much!

Acknowledgement

I would like to thank Luisito Pangilinan, A. J. Sobczak and the following individuals for their contributions to this book: Susan Weese, Gurmilap Chahal, Joe Newbert, Constance Stickler, Steve Wickens, Ambaka Hodkinson, Michael Deutch, Pawel Brodzinski, Greg Cimmarrusti, Michael Stanleigh, Randall Craig, John Cropper, Paul D. Giammalvo, Ana Maria Rodriguez, Tom Gilb, Curt Finch, Jose Moro, Willem Van Weperen, Geoff Reiss, Laurence Nicholson, Rachna Sharma, Saranjit Dosanjh, Robert Posener, Edward J. Fern, Pablo Lledó, Ronald Look, Rob Zanfardino, Val E. Cummins, Kevin Archbold, Karine Simard, Florin Gheorghiu, Derek Reinhard, Stanislaw Gasik, Conrado Morlan, Veronica Seeto, Lynda Bourne, Patrick Weaver, Dan Monselise, Ken Kruzansky, Safiya Jamal, Josh Nankivel, Naomi Caietti, Jay Khwaja, Chen Lim, Javier De La Cuba, Dina Garfinkel, Charles Seybold, Bill Thom, Jeff Hodgkinson, Rodolfo Siles, James L. Haner, Elizabeth Harrin, Walter Paul Bebirian, Iain Cruickshank, Emmanuel Rodriguez, Robert Van De Velde, Vijay Desai, Bill Crider, Aviva Davidovits, Ernani Marques da Silva, Ayman Nassar, Geoff Crane, Nic Evans and Mohammed Athif Khaleel.

Tip 1: Focus on the terrible triplets: risks, plans and business case

Pay attention to what really matters. Three project aspects—risks, plans and the business case—are tightly integrated and must be managed together. When one aspect changes, always take a good look at the others to evaluate project health and make the right decisions.

Identify, evaluate and respond to significant project risks, ranging from long-term strategic risks to short-term tactical risks and daily operational risks.

Build and actually use your project plan and its more detailed phase plans to deliver the scope of the final product successfully.

Define and work within your business case, defining benefits the project provides to the organization. If the benefits change too much, consider that it might be time to stop.

Keeping your eyes on the "terrible triplets" allows you, as a project manager, to quickly and consistently keep projects on track.

—*Susan Weese, MSPM, PMP, PgMP, PRINCE2*
Assessor/Practitioner/Instructor

Tip 2: Get in touch with the common people

Project managers understand the reality of current processes/tools and their shortcomings, and they implement new solutions or improved processes through projects. Exploring requirements or visualizing solutions mostly happens within the realms of executives, senior managers, and subject matter experts (SMEs). The grass roots are often ignored.

Make sure that you and your project team remain in touch with people at the grass roots to understand the ground realities. These can be dispatchers, order entry staff, administrative officers, and others in your area. Always have your network of people at that level. I find a technique similar to MBWA (Management by Walking Around) very handy. Go out regularly (sometimes casually) to your site of work or business area to get in touch with this network of yours.

Common sense is available with common people. Always keep in touch with them.

—Gurmilap Chahal, MEng, PMP

Tip 3: Approach project life with a healthy attitude

1. Balance life and manage stress: Balance work and idleness to increase energy. Demands never cease, so organize, prioritize and learn to say "No"! Flee, fight or flow.

2. Really get to know people: Rapport breeds trust, and trust builds solidarity. Take a genuine interest, and respect time, energy and space.

3. Listen and offer feedback: Listen with purpose. Understand them; don't expect them to understand you. Wait your turn to speak, clarify and respond.

4. Be creative: Find connections. Change your perspective. Change habits, break patterns. Oil paint. Sculpt a sandcastle. Nurture your imagination.

5. Embrace feedback and criticism. Seek it. Evaluate it. Take it for what it is. Don't take it personally. Act on it. Stay exhilarated.

Harness and build upon your talents to shape, transform, integrate disparity and influence people to embrace business change.

—*Joe Newbert, MSc*

Tip 4: Discuss all constraints at the beginning of a project

Commitment and trustfulness: If all team members have put their doubts on the table, they all feel integrated and taken seriously.

Scope: This is the best moment to reduce or enlarge the project's scope if the majority of the team thinks that should be done but is afraid to say so.

Responsibility: A shared taken decision is supported by the whole team; nobody can say "I told you it won't work."

Don't be afraid of a constructive discussion, as it will only help you in the ongoing project.

—*Constance Stickler, PM*

Tip 5: Master the art of delegation

A project manager can't know it all, or do it all. If you subscribe to the old saying that "the only way to get something done right or on time is to do it yourself," then there is a very strong likelihood that your results as a project manager will be less than stellar.

Delegation is the assignment of authority and responsibility to another person to carry out specific tasks. Such an assignment carries the accountability for execution in both a timely and an effective manner. Task assignment, however, is only half the process.

An effective project manager must follow up to ensure that assigned tasks are completed on time and in an effective manner, and must have his or her own personal tracking process for noting outstanding tasks and for executing follow-ups on those tasks.

—Steve Wickens, CAPM, PMP, PMI-RMP

Tip 6: Balance overcontrol with undercontrol

A tip from John Carver lets me think of my project as "my baby." I cradle the vision for the project. I dress my baby warmly, so I address the fundamental value for the project. As I take my baby for a stroll, I "force an external focus on value" and enable an "outcome-driven organizing system." I "separate the large issues from the small ones." When I hold my baby up for passersby to look at, I "force forward thinking" and describe relationships relevant to stakeholders. I balance overcontrol with undercontrol in order to cancel my "meddler" and "rubber stamper" tendencies.

The path to better governance lies in more productive human relationships. Think project, think baby and be the change.

—Ambaka Hodkinson

Tip 7: Go beyond "projects as usual" with mind mapping

How do you juggle hundreds of project tasks and details? Where do you put all of this information and make sense out of it, and how do you access and share it effectively?

On your next project, you could turn to the usual suspects or instead use mind maps to streamline every process, from start to finish. With mind maps, you'll bring to light all the known information and the gaps.

- Develop your work breakdown structures
- Capture and organize your research
- Solve problems and mitigate risks
- Create project dashboards
- Write reports and presentations
- Identify milestones and deliverables
- Gather requirements
- Conduct interviews
- Take project and meeting notes

Mind mapping is an easy-to-learn yet extremely powerful project visualization technique. Try it at *http://mindjet.com*.

—Michael Deutch
Chief Evangelist, Mindjet

Tip 8: Use common sense more often

We all have some kind of project management methodology. No matter how sophisticated it is, it can never fully define how to act in all conceivable situations. We often face unplanned issues. What then? One good technique is to use common sense instead of looking for ways to solve project issues "by the book."

No methodology was crafted to suit the very specific situation you're in. Acting according to schema, although safe, isn't always the best possible option. Because you normally have access to data about the issues, gather all of the facts while forgetting for a moment the limitations of your methodology. Based on the information, you can then make the best possible decision. Common sense often yields the best possible strategy. Use it whenever standard procedures don't suit your specific situation well enough.

—Pawel Brodzinski

Tip 9: Create team enthusiasm and "buy-in" by using "old school" network diagrams

Ask your project team to create the network diagram on brown butcher paper using three-inch sticky notes. This is my favorite planning methodology because it creates team unity and buy-in when everyone helps build the network diagram. I use different colors to represent different process streams. The process works like a champ for planning project cutovers.

—*Greg Cimmarrusti, PMP*

Tip 10: Stop the escalation of commitment to a failing course of action

It is a common phenomenon for stakeholders to escalate their commitment to a failing project, hoping that it will "magically" recover. Instead of propagating this fallacy, managers should undertake a project audit. By identifying and correcting the root causes of the problem, the project team can create future opportunities and savings for the organization.

- Conduct in-depth interviews with sponsors, managers, team members and vendors
- Review all documentation, including scope, detailed plan, change requests and risk assessments
- Observe team, vendor and customer meetings
- Develop a report that includes how to implement the recommendations

By performing this forensic review, the project team, the customer and the organization can steer the project back in the right direction. It does not make sense to waste resources on an initiative that is not working.

—*Michael Stanleigh*

Tip 11: Two ears and one mouth: use them in proportion

Ever wonder why children learn so quickly? And ever hear the expression "Children should be seen, and not heard"? There is a connection between these two concepts that can help us be better managers.

Consider: it is impossible to learn from others if you are the only one who is talking. This is true during a project update from your staff, while meeting your manager and even at home.

Unfortunately, some people prefer to hear themselves speak. By so doing, they unwittingly cut themselves off from key information— and the relationships needed to manage effectively. What distinguishes great managers is the quality of their listening skills.

Test yourself: what percentage of the time are you talking, instead of listening? Try setting a goal to "improve" this ratio. You have two ears and one mouth for a reason.

—Randall Craig
President, Pinetree Advisors, Inc.
Author, Online PR and Social Media for Experts *and*
Personal Balance Sheet Career Planning Guide

Tip 12: Get project governance structures in place and working effectively

Organizational politics can wreck a project. Project governance structures—a Project Board—can help. A Project Board's role is to ensure that the project achieves its anticipated benefits. Board members represent key groups. They ensure engagement with these groups, and they need to be senior enough to do this credibly and free up resources to support the project. They own risks. Above all, they ensure that the project is on track and continues to be aligned with business needs. To do this, the Project Board has to engage with the organization and its politics—on behalf of the project manager. A Project Board can be like a snowplow—it clears the way and lets you get on with managing the project.

Projects are not islands. A Project Board can help the project navigate the treacherous waters of organizational politics.

—John Cropper, MBA, PRINCE 2 Practitioner
Global Programme Manager, Oxfam GB

Tip 13: Dump clients who don't pay their bills and/or don't follow your advice

If you are a consultant or a trainer, dump clients who don't pay their bills and/or don't follow your advice. Send them to your competition. Let deadbeat clients bankrupt your competitors and blame them for failing to follow your advice.

You go to the cardiologist, and he tells you to lose 10 kilos, give up smoking and get more exercise. You don't follow his advice and you end up dying of a cardiac infarction. Who is responsible?

Clients who don't follow your advice are a danger to your reputation. Avoid them like the plague.

—*Dr. Paul D. Giammalvo*

Tip 14: Plan only details that you intend to monitor during project execution

How much detail should you put into your plan?

Do not plan details that you will not be able to monitor, or be interested in monitoring, during project execution. Do plan details that will require monitoring and controlling later. Keep in mind that you will need to get update information on them later in the project life cycle.

—*Ana Maria Rodriguez, MSE, PMP*

Tip 15: Get management to quantify the top few critical project objectives

The top-level justifications for most projects seem to be nice-sounding platitudes: impossible to interpret, to put in contracts or to measure progress against.

It is fundamental to all other aspects of a project that the primary reasons and the primary improvements (enhance, increase, reduce, improve) are spelled out unambiguously for all parties.

The big trick to achieving clarity is to quantify all change objectives.

- Define a scale of measure (Google one if your imagination fails)
- Define constraints (worst-acceptable-case numerical levels)
- Define targets (good enough levels on the scale)

I promise you: all critical seemingly soft objectives can be better expressed numerically.

Convince your top managers that their responsibility is total clarity about the reasons and expectations behind funding and supporting projects.

—Tom Gilb
Management Consultant, own company, Gilb.com
Author, Competitive Engineering

Tip 16: Track time on tasks

Farmers know their costs of production. Manufacturers know theirs. But people who produce knowledge and information outputs in our new economy—don't.

If you refuse to find out which tasks were underestimated, which projects or customers are profitable and what is currently being worked on, then very soon a competitor who does track time and does understand costs will bury you.

Worse, you will be wasting the lives and the time of many people who could be working on things the market will reward them for—things with an ROI.

—Curt Finch

Tip 17: Choose the right people

To perform the project tasks, you must assign the right people to the tasks. The right people are the people who have the skills to perform the tasks well and on time.

Creating a high-performance team is not easy. You must choose the best players for your team and lead it. During the execution of the project, new people can be incorporated, but you must ensure that they integrate into the team successfully.

—Jose Moro
CEO and Founder of gedpro –project management experts

Tip 18: Take your time to find the real problem to address

Make sure that you are addressing the right solution for the right problem. It is important to spend enough time to analyze the problem in depth and to contact the right people. The latter implies going out of your way to find them, and not to settle for those who are well known to you and who are easy to contact. By taking more time, you can develop a better understanding of the issue at stake, and the payoff to your project will be much better.

—Willem Van Weperen

Tip 19: Ask for the success criteria at the beginning of the project

At the start of every project, ask this simple question: How will I know if I did well?

You and your stakeholders must always agree on your personal measures of success right at the start.

If you and your stakeholders do not agree on your own personal measures of success, you can be certain they will have different ideas and varying expectations. It is therefore inevitable that you will disappoint some of them. It is very likely that you will let down some of the stakeholders, and it is possible that every one of them will believe you have failed.

—*Geoff Reiss*

Tip 20: Understand the project sponsor dynamics

If there is one thing that will dictate the level of difficulty that you will experience within a project, it is the level of sponsorship provided by senior management.

The more senior the sponsor, the less political the project becomes for the project manager. It remains very political, however, for the sponsor.

Establish the level of senior management buy-in early and commit to build relationships with sponsors and stakeholders in order to support and champion the initiative.

—*Laurence Nicholson, PMP*

Tip 21: Engage your team effectively in problem solving

A true case of teamwork on projects means effectively engaging your team in the process of problem solving. Although a problem could be technical, or management- or business-related, it will help if you can get multiple perspectives from different team members.

Given this, you will end up with several alternatives to arrive at a balanced solution. Moreover, you will have an engaged team who will work effectively because its members are aware of the current issues and how these issues impact their project deliverables.

My teams have a basic rule: If you have a problem, think of at least two potential solutions. If you cannot come up with at least two solutions, then think of at least one potential solution to resolve it!

—Rachna Sharma

Tip 22: Clarify your position and influence in the organization matrix

In a matrix organization, you may find that resources disappear because another project takes priority or they get assigned to other tasks. In an IT scenario, key resources may have to deal with a production system failure during a critical project activity.

You need to do two things during the planning process to address this problem.

1. Prepare a risk register and share it with stakeholders. With your project sponsor, quantify the impact of missing resources on critical path activities. Do not make vague statements such as "If I don't get the best resources, the project will be late."

2. Explore the possibility of hiring consultants on short notice. Is the learning curve short enough? What is the budget impact? Find a consultant and get a quote.

—Saranjit Dosanjh, PMP
Project Manager
PMI Belgium

Tip 23: Create a conducive work environment for the project team

- Take away all excuses for not doing a good job
- Remove roadblocks and obstacles
- Focus on the well-being of the people who are performing the work
- Allow the team to be the best that they can be
- Protect the team from those outside the team who would do it harm (deliberate or benign)
- Actively encourage and assist the project team to become a true, real team and perhaps a high-performing team

Project success is governed much more by the people aspects than by the technical aspects.

—Robert Posener
Project Manager, PMComplete Pty Ltd

Tip 24: Be honest with your sponsor and your customer

Dilemma: Being on time and within budget vs. having a happy customer and happy banker

We often hear that the criteria for a successful project should be schedule and budget performance. If, however, our objective is continued gainful employment, then these criteria simply do not matter. Only satisfied customers can sustain our employers and our employment. Look at what happened in the American auto industry and its unions.

Be honest with your sponsor and your customer. If extra time or extra money will better serve the purposes of your project, let them know this as soon as you know it. Let them make decisions based on the best information available.

—Edward J. Fern, MS, PMP

Tip 25: Improve project communications management

- Remember that people and communication come first; processes and plans come later.
- Do not communicate just by e-mail; it could be very dangerous! Try to combine some other types of communication tools such as telephone, video conference, Skype, and Webcams.
- Do not be an "easy click." Reread your e-mail before clicking "send" because someone may interpret your message differently from the way you intended.
- Open your mind to understand and communicate with your clients. They know the business much better than you.

There are two true things in life: we are going to die, and no project will be done exactly as planned. Therefore, you need a plan, but planning is an iterative process that requires effective communication.

—Pablo Lledó, PMP

Tip 26: Communicate, communicate and communicate

And when you are done with that, double-check to ensure that you did not miss anybody!

How many project reviews have had a finding that noted that the cause of a problem was communications? Even knowing this, we repeat this mistake over and over again.

It seems so simple, but it's not. Communication must be timely. Communication that is too late or too early will lose most of its pertinence. Yes, you can communicate something too early.

True communication is a two-way street. If you sent an e-mail copying the world, it does not mean you communicated. If your audience did not understand the message, then all you did was send an e-mail. You may have to follow up with key recipients. Following up, oh the horror!
Communication is to project management what location is to real estate!

—*Ronald Look*

Tip 27: Move everyone in one direction

If you know where people are coming from, you know where they are going.

As a project manager, you need to move everyone in one direction. That may be your agenda, but it may not necessarily be shared by all of your project team members. The Black Pen Concept© says that if you were to present an object such as a black pen to a group, some would some call it black and some would call it dark grey. How can two different people look at the same information and derive different viewpoints? The Black Pen Concept© identifies that we create our conclusions or derive our decisions about work and life based on our experiences.

As a project manager, you need to know where individuals are coming from to get them where you need them to go.

—*Rob Zanfardino*

Tip 28: Ensure that you have an open door policy

What is an open door policy? An open door policy does not mean announcing that YOU have an open door—very few people will cross the doorstep and talk to the boss; and those that do—maybe you don't want to talk to them.

An open door policy is when you get up from your desk and walk around to the desks and cubicles of your project team members. Open THEIR doors and do MBWA (Management by Walking Around).
You get the pulse, you see the motivation and you feel the energy and commitment of your team. You also get to make a difference—ask them what bothers them, what keeps them up at night and what they feel good about. And, you get to HELP!

—Val E. Cummins

Tip 29: Manage your stakeholders' expectations

Many projects are deemed to have failed even though the project manager believes he/she did a reasonable job. How is this possible? Because one or more of the stakeholders expected the project deliverables to be different from what was produced. In other words, they were surprised in some way by the outcome—and in business, people generally don't like to be surprised. Even if the deliverables perform wonderfully, if they're not what people are expecting, those people will get upset. So identify all your stakeholders, clarify and set their expectations and then manage those expectations throughout the life of the project.

You may not be able to meet all their requirements, but you certainly can manage all their expectations.

—Kevin Archbold

Tip 30: Relax—the world is not about to explode

You are the project team's leader. How you feel about the project will be reflected in how your team works. If you are anxious about delivering the project on time and on budget, the team will feel your anxiety—which may not improve the quality of their work.

Remember:

- How you feel about a project CAN change how the project goes.
- Adopt a positive attitude, even when things go wrong. You will see a change in your team's effectiveness.
- You and your team are HUMANS, not machines. Treat yourself and your team accordingly.

The emotions and attitude you bring to your team directly influence the quality they give back to the project.

—Karine Simard, PMP
Project Manager, Websystems Inc.

Tip 31: Ensure that the project charter has your name on it

The most important tip that I can offer, looking back from my past bitter experience, is to make sure that the project charter explicitly states your appointment as the project manager and that it is released by an executive in your organization.

All bad and good things start from a project manager who is not instated formally and empowered with good leverage to act at full capacity without being afraid at any moment that certain limits are exceeded.

You cannot be yourself from the moment of kickoff unless the project team, the sponsor and all other stakeholders recognize and accept you and your binding decisions on the project course.

Before any proceeding, one has to be sure that the project charter and the project manager appointment are formally released.

—Florin Gheorghiu, MPM, PMP

Tip 32: Integrate (don't get enamoured with) technology

1. There are many PM applications (and many non-PM applications that work just fine for PM). Use what you know and know will work.

2. Help yourself, your team, your stakeholders and your customer by presenting a consistent "look and feel" in reports and other output.

3. Even if you think it's the coolest tool/application, if it requires others to spend a lot of time learning how it works, keep it to yourself.

4. If you are going to use a new tool/application, frontload the training—and (a) tell your users why it's important to learn it for this project and (b) get the training done before the project starts. It is suboptimal to ask your team or stakeholders to learn something "on the fly" while supporting the project.

—Derek Reinhard

Tip 33: Know the true meaning of project management

1. You always have to know the real goal of the project. Many project stakeholders have their own goals, but remember that you are hired (or employed) by the organization responsible for the project and you are obliged to work just toward its goals. If you want to work toward other goals, you may establish your own company and work for it.

2. Project management means people management. Remember that everything you do depends on people managed by you. Project success is the success of your people. And never call people "a resource." They are human beings.

3. Project management does not mean document management. You have to document many things, but producing documentation is not your basic job. Your basic job is just making decisions and assuming responsibility for these decisions.

—Stanislaw Gasik

Tip 34: Use the "Chinese Army Approach" when scoping project resources

As a project manager, you will need to identify the resources to be included in the different tasks of the project. This activity may turn difficult and may become a roadblock in the selection process.

My recommendation is to use the "Chinese Army Approach," which literally has unlimited resources, and assign roles or skills required instead of names of resources.

When this activity is completed, the project manager will have scoped all the required resources and then will be able to identify the internal resources that can fulfill the role or the skill; and those that cannot be fulfilled can be sourced from other groups or vendors.

—Conrado Morlan

Tip 35: Own the project and don't be a slave to the project plan schedule

Although it is important to have a project plan schedule to track progress, this should not be your only focus!

Remember that you are managing a project with people, processes and deliverables. Sometimes we get caught up in the project schedule and think that following the project plan tasks means that we are doing a good job. Keeping busy updating and completing tasks does not mean it is a successful project with a quality result.

You own the project, and the schedule is only a tool to monitor progress. Talk to people, walk around and find out what is going on with people. Make decisions based on their input and feedback.

Keep a pulse on the project and listen to people. Don't let the project plan drive you.

—Veronica Seeto
HRIS Test Coordinator, Toronto District School Board

Tip 36: Understand who's who and who's playing

Projects attract stakeholders. You need to find out who they are and manage their relationships with the project if you want to succeed.

Only when you understand who the important stakeholders are can you develop and implement a structured communication plan to positively influence their attitudes and expectations. Your stakeholder community is never static! People's attitudes change, and individual stakeholders become more or less important as time goes by. Routine monitoring is critical, supported by adjustments to your communication plan.

If this sounds hard, it is a lot less difficult than dealing with a failed project, and help is at hand. Take a look at *http://stakeholder-management.com* for a range of resources to support the Stakeholder Circle® methodology. This lets you focus on the right stakeholders at the right time to maximize your chances of success.

—Dr. Lynda Bourne, DPM, PMP
Managing Director, Stakeholder Management Pty Ltd

Tip 37: Treat your schedule as king

Useful schedules are used! The only thing management can influence is the future; the past is a fact, and the present is too late.

Useful schedules are developed collaboratively, are used to coordinate the work of the project team and help management formulate wise decisions. Good schedules are:

- Elegant and easy to understand
- Concise and accurate
- As simple as possible
- Maintained by regular status/updates—all incomplete work MUST be in the future!

To achieve these objectives, you must avoid vast schedules and unnecessary detail—no one understands them, and you can't maintain them; for guidance refer to the PMI Practice Standard for Scheduling. Only after you understand the flow and timing of the work can you hope to develop accurate resource plans and then cost budgets.

—Patrick Weaver, PMP, PMI-SP
Managing Director, Mosaic Project Services Pty Ltd

Tip 38: Manage expectations

When it comes to getting a task or a project done, it is always better to under-promise and over-deliver than it is to over-promise and under-deliver.

—Dan Monselise, MBA, CISSP

Tip 39: Do NOT let technology overwhelm reality when planning a project

The design, scope and level of technology to be deployed must take into account the actual end user of any project. Do NOT be enticed into the idea that a one-button system can be implemented. These systems do not exist.

If the actual end users of a project, either a new implementation or an upgrade of an existing system, are not able to functionally use and understand the new system, the result will be less-than-expected usage and acceptance.

—Ken Kruzansky, MBA

Tip 40: Deal with politics in the workplace

Politics shape our lives and the workplace, yet a lot of us would prefer not to get too entangled in them. The reality, however, is that in project management, more than in any other area of specialization, the success of your project depends on how well you navigate through the eccentricities of those in power.

- Get to know the "political" team members by using work or social opportunities to understand their personality and behavior and what's important to them

- Understand what drives them and how you can partner with them so that they can support you and help deliver aspects of the project
- Be in regular touch with these members, as they are the grapevine and what they say often does shape team dynamics and possibly influence the outcome of the project
- Keep your sense of humor and yourself intact through it all

Politics are real, so as a project manager, you must deal with them effectively and "keep on trucking."

—Safiya Jamal
All About Words

Tip 41: Put the horse in front of the cart

- Do things in the right order
- Ask yourself "What are the prerequisites for us to do this the RIGHT way?"
- When asked to do things out of order, push back and hold your ground
- Resist the temptation to say "OK, we'll do it, but it won't be any good."
- Ask trusted outsiders if you are too involved with the chaos to tell what is the right order

This is easier when you are in the planning phases, and much more difficult when you are doing a re-plan while work is going on. Either way, it's critical.

—Josh Nankivel, PMP

Tip 42: Be a STAR (Self-starter Taking Action Right now)

- Raise the value proposition in your organization by focusing on the customer first, and producing quality results and outcomes.
- Choose the right fit of methodologies (e.g., PMBOK/Agile) at the right time for the right customer.
- Focus on your own personal growth and development as a leader—soft/hard skills.
- Adjust your leadership style accordingly. Are your teams a mix of Millennials, GenXers, Boomers or Traditionalists? If so, consider how you communicate with and acknowledge your project teams.
- Make change leadership a focus for your projects and organization.
- Get involved: volunteer for a community of practice, special interest group or other networking group.
- Help raise the awareness of project management leadership in your organization and advance the profession one day at a time.

—Naomi Caietti, PMP
Enterprise Architect/Project Manager

Tip 43: Begin with stakeholders' approval and keep them engaged

- The stakeholders, especially the senior management, play a key role in determining the success of the project. Try to keep them happy.
- Be careful in picking the methodology to run the project. If it is overkill, the project can get into shambles. Select the methodology based on the size, duration, budget and complexity of the project, with careful assessment of organizational maturity on programs and practices.
- Keep the communications flowing to all work areas in the project, including those that have completed their portions.

- No project is simple, easy or impossible. There are always unique situations, but good solutions normally come from within an organization—and that solution is always easy to sell.
- Recognize and reward the team for completing major milestones to keep spirits high.

—Jay Khwaja

Tip 44: Manage your project risks

Identify, categorize, resolve and review the project risks throughout the project life cycle.

—Chen Lim

Tip 45: Choose one approach and plan accordingly

When managing a project that requires you to implement a software solution, there are essentially three alternative approaches that you must choose from:

Alternative 1: Adopt, not adapt—implement the solution as is and stick to it

Alternative 2: Adopt, then adapt—implement the solution as is first, then change it as required

Alternative 3: Adopt and adapt—ensure you understand the risks involved and plan accordingly. If possible, reconsider alternatives 1 and 2.

These three alternatives are mutually exclusive. Alternatives 1 and 3 require strong business leadership and clarity on intent and scope; make sure you have both.

If you must choose Alternative 3, be very careful and plan even more carefully.

—*Javier De La Cuba*

Tip 46: Plan early and often!

"If you don't have time to do it right, when do you have time to do it over?"

Too often, we forsake early and thorough planning because we want to jump right into the project. It is only once we're in the middle of things that questions come up that slow things down, or worse, team members without the right information are left to make their own decisions about specific elements of the project and easily make the wrong ones.

Invest time in the beginning to plan and document as much of the project as possible. Never hesitate to stop in the middle if questions arise, and take the time to figure things out.

—*Dina Garfinkel, PMP*

Tip 47: Cut early and cut often!

An excess inventory of unmade decisions is nothing to which you should aspire. Unmade decisions increase the drag on project efficiency and introduce uncertainty that clouds the true picture of the project. You can always add a little something in at the last minute, but trying to take things out late in the game is the worst.

—*Charles Seybold*

Tip 48: Wrap project requirements around quality

When taking the time to gather project requirements, take the time to identify the quality expectations of the customer.

We are all people with different types of thought processes; our individual thoughts and expectations differ from those of others around us. In order to write good requirements, take the time to capture the quality your customer expects. Convey that message to the team, and design to those requirements.

Take the time to meet the customer's requirements and their quality expectations, and you will see more project success.

—*Bill Thom, PMP*

Tip 49: Always have one agreed-upon project approach

After completing the documentation of your project scope and before you begin to build a project schedule, have an "approach" discussion with your project team. What is "key" is to agree to a defined "how" the project will be implemented. Once the approach is agreed to by the entire team, the project schedule will be of higher confidence and clarity. There will also be less potential for changes over the life cycle of the project.

In discussing the approach with your team, ensure that you will not discuss the time it takes to do the work but instead list the logical "steps" of how the project needs to be done.

—*Jeff Hodgkinson, MBA, PMP, PgMP, PME, IPMA-B*

Tip 50: Perform "After Action Reviews" after key milestones

Project managers need to make a habit of incorporating a process of lessons learning during the life of the project and not only at its end. Lessons learning means that at each key milestone, the project makes a stop to review assumptions, evaluate changes in the internal and external environment and review risks and estimates. The idea is to adapt the project plans to any changes that will impact the final objective. An analogy is driving a car using a map that doesn't take in consideration changes in the road due to construction, accident and detours. Plans should be taken not as written in stone but as estimates that require updates on a frequent basis.

"Planning is useless, but planning is essential"—Eisenhower.

—Rodolfo Siles, MScM, PMP

Tip 51: Use a to-do list

Create your to-do list by brainstorming everything you need to do in the day and writing it on the list. Don't worry if you end up with a long list.

Your to-do list should be

- Created new for each day. Writing your tasks down unloads your psychic RAM. When you don´t occupy your mind with having to remember everything, it becomes easier to think clearly.
- Kept in immediate view at all times. Seeing your list throughout the day keeps you on track when you may want to do less important, low-priority tasks.
- Carried with you wherever you go. You can use your to-do list to bring clarity about relative urgency and importance.

If you are working on a big project, the to-do list can motivate you by letting you see how much you've really done.

—*James L. Haner, PMP, PgMP*

Tip 52: Do not be afraid to speak up

The average large company, running around 150 projects at any one time, loses £13 million a year by not stopping projects that are failing. It's not always management's responsibility to cancel projects. If you're working on something that you know isn't going to deliver the proposed benefits, you need to speak up.

The project manager's role is partly to direct the work and partly to provide an objective position on how the work is done—and that means suggesting stopping everything and starting again, or even not starting again, if necessary.

Don't be afraid to challenge senior people. Not all projects are started from the basis of a competent idea. If you know the project is going to fail, explain why it should be stopped. It is up to your sponsor to make the final decision to stop it.

—*Elizabeth Harrin, MA, PRINCE2 Practitioner*
Author, Project Management in the Real World

Tip 53: Learn how to delegate

Leave yourself enough space to see the entire picture.

—*Walter Paul Bebirian*

Tip 54: Spend as much time analyzing the project team as you do the project requirements

Many project teams are made up of culturally diverse and/or virtually located resources. It is becoming more and more important for a project manager to spend time learning about the individuals who make up the project team.

The lack of face-to-face meetings, the inability to "walk down the hall" for a chat and the different cultural backgrounds can make it difficult for a project manager to provide direction and receive needed feedback.

A project manager needs to ensure that his/her communication with the team equals or exceeds the communication with non-team stakeholders.

—Iain Cruickshank, PMP

Tip 55: Never base your project plan on best-case estimates

Often, as project managers, we don't give proper instructions to SMEs on how to give proper estimates.

Risks must be taken into account when making estimates at all levels of the project. At the activity level, risks can be taken into account using the formula $(P + 4M + O)/6$, where P = pessimistic, M = most likely and O = optimistic estimates. At the project level, overall identified risks must be taken into account and added to cost as a project contingency. Lastly, at the management level, a reserve must be added to the overall cost to account for unidentified risks.

Accounting for risk builds realistic estimates, and realistic estimates are a backbone of realistic project plans.

—Emmanuel Rodriguez

Tip 56: Always give credit where it's due

The project manager is the voice of the project. That makes it easy for people outside the project team to get the wrong impression. They can think that the one who voices the ideas, insights and solutions related to the project is the one who came up with them.

To be sure, a good project manager produces a fair share of breakthrough contributions, but a good team produces far more. It may be tempting for the project manager to bask in the glow of the false impression, to let it stand. That temptation must be resisted.

The best way to stifle a team's creativity, to dam the flow of results, is to take credit for others' work. Conversely, the best way to promote a team's creativity, to encourage the flow of results, is to always give credit where it's due.

—Robert Van De Velde

Tip 57: Use lessons learned; don't reinvent the wheel

Lessons learned are a way to learn from the experiences of others, thus reducing the time others spend solving problems. Use lessons learned to:

- Improve the quality and productivity of work requests
- Reduce repetition of errors and missteps
- Provide a foundation for evaluating and improving activities
- Support continuous learning and process improvement
- Allow associates to contribute to the improvement of others, a project or an organization

As an example, IBM is shifting the organization toward a culture based on open and frequent communication with employees who are more proactive in identifying and acting on improvement opportunities.

Turn "Lessons Learned" into "Lessons Applied." Don't reinvent, re-use! Lessons Learned are not learned if not executed.

—Vijay Desai, PMP

Tip 58: Engage coaches to improve performance

One team member is not meeting deadlines or performance expectations. You determine that the problem is not overtasking or lack of commitment, but insufficient skills or motivation. What should you do?

A replacement may be difficult to find and would need time to "spin up" on the project. Furthermore, the team member will lose esteem and the project may be further delayed. A better course might be to enlist a coach.

Find someone with the right skill set to provide coaching and encouragement. The coach should not do the work but should provide motivational and technical advice to help the team member excel in the future.

Everyone wins: the team member becomes productive for this and future projects, the project gets back on schedule and the coach gets recognition for his or her efforts.

—Bill Crider, PMP
Senior Global Project Manager
Intel Corporation

Tip 59: Encourage your project team to share ideas

People are the most important resource in your project. They usually have great ideas that can solve hard issues. They are smart and can look at the problem from a different angle. Trust them.

—Aviva Davidovits
Global Project Manager
Intel Corporation

Tip 60: Focus on the end state

When working on a project, even if a small one, it is very common to get confused in the large amounts of information and situations that appear. You should maintain your focus in the solution and coach your team to behave in the same way.

This can be achieved when the information is organized, the solution is clear, the vision of the end state is commonly shared and the team is motivated to get the work done.

Difficult situations will pop up during the project life cycle, and if the dynamic of finding the solution is well disseminated among the team and the stakeholders, the success of the project will be easier to achieve.

—Ernani Marques da Silva, MBA, PMP, PgMP
PMO—Citibank Brasil

Tip 61: Listen more than you talk

Project managers are inherent leaders. You need to inspire your team to work harder to accomplish more work for less cost and better quality. Listen to the team's concerns, their understanding of the value of the project, its significance and their role in the bigger picture. Make sure your team is immersed in the mission of the project.

Listening skills for a project manager are crucial for effective communication across the project. Make sure messages relayed to the team by self or others are (1) clear, (2) accurate, (3) relevant, (4) concise, (5) at the correct level of detail and (6) transmitted using the most effective medium.

—Ayman Nassar, MSc Eng Mgmt, MSc EE, PMP, CSEP, CSSGB
IT Architect & Systems Engineer—IBM Corporation
Project Management Faculty—Prince George's Community College
Board of Directors, Chair—Islamic Leadership Institute of America

Tip 62: Make sure that you trust your core message

Establish a climate of trust on your project. This is a practice-what-you-preach concept, so it has to start with you.

Build Trust

- Make an effort to get to know your team and your stakeholders.
- Make a point of being trustworthy with every decision you make and every response you give.
- Lead by example. Let your team know how to behave by watching how you behave.

Manage Trust

- Build a communications plan so you know your team is building important relationships effectively.
- Set an open door policy. You want people to come to you with problems.
- Encourage trustworthiness in your people. Don't punish them for making mistakes or bringing you bad news.

—Geoff Crane

Tip 63: Keep your plans agile and objectives personal

Your project plans need to be detailed for the near term so that everyone knows:

- What they are working on,
- What their accountability is for the deliverables and quality and
- How this fits into the greater objective.

The only thing that is certain about a long-term detailed plan is that it will be wrong. PMs can learn a lot from military strategy—a general doesn't plan a battle in detail but depends on soldiers knowing their objectives, so they can react to events and seize opportunities.

"A good plan violently executed now is better than a perfect plan executed next week."—General George S. Patton

—Nic Evans

Tip 64: Identify, record, track and resolve issues

Issues are bound to occur in projects. Issues can arise within the project team/performing organization, project sponsor, stakeholders, customers, vendors, etc. A project manager should identify, record, track and resolve issues using the issue log throughout the project. Failure to resolve issues might affect project delivery.

Enforce a deadline to resolve the issues and to achieve a WIN-WIN outcome.

—*Mohammed Athif Khaleel*

Tip 65: Use the three E's when dealing with difficult people

Christine Comaford-Lynch's book *Rules for Renegades* (p. 174) talks about how to deal with difficult people. I found her advice useful, so I decided to share it here.

Equalize: Place yourself on par with the person in your mind. You both were drooling babies; you both will grow old and die; you both are made of the same stuff.

Exchange: Perhaps the person is suffering in some aspect of life. Maybe this is why the individual is so difficult to deal with. Remember a time when you were struggling and "exchange" your suffering for his or hers.

Embrace: Accept people exactly as they are. When you are annoyed by people's behaviors, know that you cannot possibly change them, so embrace or accept people just as they are. Later on, you can decide to interact with them or not.

—*Adapted from Christine Comaford-Lynch,*
Rules for Renegades

Tip 66: Prevent project scope creep using the seven steps

Prevent undocumented and/or unapproved changes by strictly adhering to fundamental scope management and change request (CR) processes.

Unless there is an approved CR, do not allow changes on signed-off documents.

From Requirements to Solution

1. Requirements Document (RD): gather requirements; conduct walkthroughs; prepare the final version; get sign-offs
2. Traceability: trace the proposed design (PD) against the RD (items not mentioned in the RD should not be in the PD); get signoffs
3. Acceptance Checklist (AC): create based on RD and PD; get sign-offs before starting solution development
4. Actual Solution (product, service or result): accept only if it meets RD, PD and AC parameters

Change Request Process

5. Establish a change control board (CCB)
6. Submit all CRs to the CCB for "approval to estimate"
7. CCB to approve, defer or reject the CR based on the estimated impacts

Tip 67: Apply religious concepts to project team building

Although some people may not believe in religions, we can definitely apply what Fr. Ed Murphy learned from a Jewish Cantor. Similar to religions, project team building requires three components: belonging, believing and becoming.

Popular motivational theories consider a sense of belonging as a key motivational factor. Team members need to feel that they are part of the project in order for them get a sense of "personal ownership, responsibility and commitment."

Team members will believe in a project only if they feel that they are part of it. It cannot be forced upon someone. It can only grow through communication, collaboration and conflict resolution.

"Becoming" can be fostered by experiencing a sense of a belonging and believing in the project objectives. You will know that you have a well-built team when they start preaching the project benefits to others.

Tip 68: Deliver projects as promised: Stick to the baseline or manage through change requests

The preliminary project scope statement outlines the project and product objectives, along with high-level scope, schedule and budget. Requirements collections help refine various parameters that often serve as the initial project baseline.

Given that several unknowns will materialize as you progress deeper into the project, what is the best way to deal with them? Despite your best project management plan, you may have no choice but to issue change requests to address the changing project dynamics.

Is it better to do everything in your power to stick to the initial baseline or succumb to the need to issue change requests? With the former, you will look good by keeping your promise but may end up delivering an inadequate product. With the latter, you run the risk of losing your credibility by not delivering as promised.

What should you do?

Tip 69: Clarify the "the ask"—a management tool to expedite tasks

From various engagements, consultants get to see the best practices of top organizations worldwide. A good tool or technique usually becomes part of the consultant's repertoire of best practices.

In the last few months, I have learned the concept of "the ask." In a project, you need to have a clear understanding of the "project sponsor's ask." What is it that s/he is asking you to deliver?

When delegating tasks to team members, be explicit on what you are "asking" them to do. Do you want them to review the documents and provide feedback, or do you want them to edit and finalize the documents?

Instead of simply forwarding an e-mail with an FYI, tell them what to do with it—"no action is needed" or "add a calendar reminder."

A clear "ask" can expedite the completion of tasks.

Tip 70: Remember project management tasks in exactly three words

The *PMBOK® Guide* uses 459 pages to document the project management body of knowledge. Inspired by Dharmesh Shah's *Startup Advice in Exactly Three Words*, the list of tasks below, in rough sequence, captures the essence of a project manager's job.

Initiating

- Develop the charter
- Identify all stakeholders

Planning

- Collect high-level requirements
- Define the scope
- Determine the budget
- Prepare the schedule
- Plan for quality
- Build the team
- Prepare a communication plan
- Manage project risks
- Plan project procurements

Executing, Monitoring and Controlling

- Schedule weekly meetings
- Assemble a steering committee
- Keep monitoring risks
- Ensure project quality
- Recognize good work
- Resolve issues quickly
- Adjust plans accordingly
- Communicate potential problems
- Motivate the team

Closing

- Close all contracts
- Capture lessons learned

Tip 71: Implement the four-step process for peak performance and productivity

The four-step process below incorporates concepts from *Getting Things Done* (David Allen), twice-daily e-mail checks from *The 4-*

Hour Workweek (Tim Ferriss) and techniques that I have been using successfully for several years.

1. Take control of your e-mails using eight easy steps to eliminate e-mails (Tip 72). Process your e-mails only twice a day, once at mid-morning to respond to overnight and early morning e-mails, and again at mid-afternoon.

2. Transform the e-mails in your Do folder into one-line action items: use the verb-noun format, e.g., "Read the report."

3. Prioritize your action items using three tricks for tackling top tasks (Tip 82).

4. Apply assembly-line techniques: work on one group of top tasks at a time by location (home, office or away) and tools (computer, phone, etc.)

Tip 72: Exercise the eight easy ways to eliminate e-mails

Learn how to get rid of unnecessary e-mails in your inbox!

These steps are based on Outlook but also can be done with other e-mail programs.

1. Create five folders: Do, Defer, Delegate, Document and Delete (Dr. Estrella's "Deadly D Directories")
2. Group related e-mails by sorting them by subject
3. Review each e-mail and decide
4. If an action is needed today, move it to the Do folder
5. If no immediate action is needed, move it to Defer (right-click on the message, point to Follow Up and then click on Add Reminder)
6. If someone else should do it, Delegate it and add a reminder
7. If the e-mail contains useful information, move it to the Document folder

8. If you cannot decide, move it to Delete

Prioritize the Do folder daily. Revisit the rest weekly.

Tip 73: Learn from your mistakes: Nine reasons why project failures are good

Project failures are good only if you can learn from your mistakes. With a keen eye on lessons learned and failure points, here are nine potential ways to turn a project failure into future project successes.

1. Design a case study around it
2. Update organizational procedures
3. Institute new preventive policies
4. Add an item in the risk checklist
5. Document symptoms of the failure points
6. Create a gate-driven diagnostic tool
7. Revise project management training manuals
8. Train staff on how to prevent similar problems
9. Use as a basis for quantifying project failures

There are times when you can learn more from your project failures than from your project successes. As long as you keep your mistakes small by making them early, you can use them to become a better project manager.

Tip 74: Earn project management certifications for the right reasons

Don't bother with earning project management certifications if your primary reasons include getting instant fame and fortune. Consider getting a project management certification only if you are willing to:

*   Change your old habits
*   Standardize your terminologies

- Learn additional tools and techniques
- Commit to professional development

And if your organization will agree to:

- Change ineffective and inefficient processes
- Aspire to consistent and repeatable results
- Reward your efforts based on project results
- Expect that success will not happen overnight

It takes two to tango. Likewise, certifications are valuable only with mutual commitments. If you can't tango or get your organization to dance along, you might as well not give it a go!

Tip 75: Unlock the 19 secrets to make project management effective and efficient

Project management will remain ineffective and inefficient unless:

The project sponsor

1. Gives a clear project objective
2. Helps craft a well-defined project scope
3. Removes project obstacles
4. Mediates disagreements
5. Supports the project team

Customers or end-users

6. Help refine the project scope
7. Convey requirements fully and clearly
8. Avoid changing their minds frequently
9. Adhere to the change management process

Subject-matter experts

10. Highlight common pitfalls
11. Help vs. hinder decision making

The project team

12. Buys in to the project objective
13. Identifies all required tasks
14. Provides accurate estimates
15. Reports progress truthfully
16. Delivers their commitments
17. Focuses on business value vs. technical features

The project manager

18. Recognizes that there is no "I" in project
19. Resolves issues and risks that may arise from the 18 items above quickly, efficiently and effectively.

Tip 76: Create visual project timelines

Consider using Microsoft Visio if you need to quickly put together a high-level timeline to share with your project sponsors and team members. If needed, you can easily embed the visual timeline into a regular document or a presentation slide deck.

In Visio 2003, on the File menu, point to New, point to Project Schedule and click on Timeline.

In Visio 2007, Project Schedule is simply called Schedule.

Drag the block, line, ruler, divided or cylindrical timeline into the drawing area.

Add a bracket, block or cylindrical interval as appropriate.

If needed, add an expanded timeline to provide more details to a portion of the timeline.

Jazz up your timeline by adding milestones (diamond, square, circle, X, triangle, 2 triangle, line, pin or cylindrical).

Tip 77: Generate gorgeous Gantt charts

Did you know that you can generate gorgeous Gantt charts using Microsoft Visio?

Although it is fairly easy to create Gantt charts in Microsoft Project, it is too time-consuming to "pretty it up" for executive presentations. In contrast, you can easily change the backgrounds, borders, titles and other features in Microsoft Visio.

In Visio 2003, on the File menu, point to New, point to Project Schedule and then click on Gantt Chart.

In Visio 2007, Project Schedule is simply called Schedule.

Click on OK in the Gantt Chart Options dialog box.

If you need to import an existing Microsoft Project file, follow the steps above but click on Cancel when prompted in the Gantt Chart Options dialog box.

On the Gantt Chart menu, click on Import to invoke the Import Project Data Wizard. Follow the steps in the wizard.

Tip 78: Understand the need to be "cool" under pressure

At the Canadian Association of Professional Speakers' (CAPS) National Convention in Calgary, I unfortunately missed an item in the checklist. That resulted in there being no screen and projector when I showed up 15 minutes prior to my presentation.

As a project manager, I thrive under pressure, so I did not panic. What I found most commendable was how the meeting organizers (Shari Bricks and her team, and Impact Entertainment) handled the situation. During the entire ordeal, they remained calm, and we were able to start as if nothing happened.

We can learn several lessons from this incident. People are people. They make mistakes. Regardless of how many checklists and plans you may have, issues will still arise. What is important is to focus on what you can control—issue resolution—and your emotions and reactions to tough situations.

Tip 79: Wow project team members with words that change minds

Shelle Rose Charvet is the author of *Words That Change Minds*. As an expert in below-consciousness communication processes, she talks about "toward" and "away" types of communication in her keynote speeches.

"Toward" focuses on achieving goals such as staying within budget or even trying to lose weight. In contrast, "away" deals with preventing problems (moving away from), such as asking for additional funding or being called obese.

Unfortunately, some people are not motivated by "toward" words, so if you are not getting any response on your "RED" project status, it might be worthwhile to adjust your communication style to the "away" format.

Consider saying "We will pay a huge penalty if we deliver late" vs. "Deliver on time to get your bonus." "Die prematurely and not see your grandchildren" might be a better motivator than "eat healthy to stay fit."

—Adapted from Shelle Rose Charvet,
Words That Change Minds

Tip 80: Fix resource overallocation

After entering all of the tasks in project management software, look at your resource allocation. Sometimes, it is better to address overallocations before publishing the project schedule instead of asking your team members to work overtime down the road.

1. Delay the task: Look for slack in the schedule to determine if you can reschedule the task without affecting the critical path.
2. Split the task: Similar to delaying the task, but only for a portion of it.
3. Don't do the task: Is the task a need or a want? If the latter, then either put it out of scope or move it to another phase.
4. Get additional resources: Depending on the project constraints, additional resources can help reduce the overallocation.
5. Use experienced resources: If possible, replace junior resources with experienced staff to finish tasks faster.

Tip 81: Learn the four project management calendars

Base Calendar: Serves as a template for project, resource and task calendars. Basic format includes Standard (8:00 A.M. to 5:00 P.M., one hour for lunch and off on weekends), 24 Hours and Night Shift. Adjust the base calendar if your company works fewer than 40 hours per week. Statutory holidays can also be defined in the Base Calendar.

Project Calendar: Documents the start and end dates in the project. In a manufacturing setting, you can set plant shutdowns on this calendar.

Resource Calendar: Captures nonworking hours of a resource such as vacation and training. Use this calendar to indicate nontraditional working hours as well as night shifts.

Task Calendar: Helps adjust working times for nonhuman resources such as machines that must run overnight or 24 hours daily.

By setting these calendars correctly, project management software can calculate task durations correctly.

Tip 82: Tackle top tasks using these three tricks

Use the UID Technique, Rule of 1/3 and Huge Hurdle Method to tackle your top tasks.

1. UID Technique (Urgency, Importance and Delegate): Assign "urgency" and "importance" numerical values to each task on your tasks list. A simple 1, 2 and 3 for low, medium and high respectively will suffice. Multiply the urgency and importance factors to determine the task's priority. Sort the priorities in descending order. The delegate component prompts you to decide if a task should be delegated.

2. Rule of 1/3: Designate 1/3 of your tasks as low, 1/3 as medium and 1/3 as high. You may apply this rule to urgency and/or importance factors.

3. Huge Hurdle Method: Break what appears to be an "insurmountable task" into smaller, less procrastination-prone tasks. Think of it as a Work Breakdown Structure (WBS) for tasks instead of projects.

Tip 83: Apply the eight project management task constraints

The most common task constraint, As Soon As Possible (ASAP), works for most dependencies. Essentially, by default, Task B will start immediately after the completion of Task A. Project managers can use seven other task constraints when creating the schedule.

1. As Late As Possible (ALAP): tasks must end at the same time as the project finish
2. Finish No Earlier Than (FNET): tasks must finish on or after a specific date
3. Finish No Later Than (FNLT): tasks must finish on or before a specific date
4. Must Finish On (MFO): tasks must finish on a specific date
5. Must Start On (MSO): tasks must start on a specific date
6. Start No Earlier Than (SNET): tasks must start on or after a specific date
7. Start No Later Than (SNLT): tasks must start on or before a specific date

Tip 84: Regain control of a failing project using the three-step project recovery process

In orienteering, you need to know where you are and where you need to go in order to succeed. The same principles apply when rescuing troubled projects.

First, determine what's causing the problem on your project. Are there financial issues? Are there unresolved decisions? What are the outstanding tasks? Was an assumption invalidated? Did a risk materialize? List all of the issues in as much detail as you can.

Second, confirm if the project objective is still valid. With the passage of time, economic changes and other factors, project sponsors may have changed their expectations and your project team therefore may still be marching toward an objective that is now obsolete.

Third, with your starting and ending points known, identify what needs to be done to bring you closer to your destination. Adjust your project management plan as appropriate.

Tip 85: Let the project team run the project

There is an incorrect and dangerous notion that project managers must "know it all, do it all." Because of the complexities of financial, technological, logistical and political components of most projects, it is unrealistic to expect project managers to be "superheroes."

Given this, it is incumbent for project managers to focus on their key role, that is, to create an environment so that all team members can excel in delivering the project objectives as outlined in the project charter.

Don't try to please everybody. Don't get caught up with the project politics.

Delegate responsibilities. Let the team make decisions. Let the subject matter experts resolve their issues. Clarify inconsistencies. Facilitate communication. Remove red tape. Align tasks to people's interests and expertise. Provide encouragement. Give pats on the back. Lastly, ensure that you and the project team are having fun!

Tip 86: Convey constructive criticisms to colleagues

You may have been noticed a colleague's quirks. They may be small, such as a loud giggle or a strong perfume. Other annoyances may include bad breath, nose hairs, body odors or uncoordinated outfits.

These idiosyncrasies can be career ending for your colleague. How do you break the bad news, in a caring way, to help turn things around?

In a private setting and using a genuinely sincere tone of voice, use this sentence from *The Practical Coach* video: "At times, your _____ are too noticeable." Read the sentence carefully. "At times" implies that it doesn't happen all the time. The adverb "too" elevates the problem without making it too harsh.

Hopefully, your colleague will do something about the problem. You may hurt his or her feelings, but if you don't point out the problem, who will?

—Video available at
http://owenstewart.com/training_videos/view/the-practical-coach

Tip 87: Be careful when dealing with difficult co-workers

When you point a finger at someone, remember that three fingers are pointing back at you. You can use the same metaphor when dealing with difficult co-workers.

Before you blame a "difficulty" solely on your co-workers, ask the following questions. Have I listened more than I talked? Have I made attempts to understand them? Have I been tolerant enough? Am I sending signals that make my co-workers react the way they do?

Second, it is prudent to check your feelings with a trusted colleague prior to approaching your difficult co-workers. When you do, do so privately.

Be very honest and precise about "your difficulty"—personal hygiene, aggressive behavior, condescending comments, constant complainers, missed deadlines, etc. Get acknowledgments from the other parties and agree on specific mutual changes to improve the situation. Schedule a follow-up meeting as needed.

Tip 88: Prevail with personal project portfolio management

Project portfolio management (PPM) enables organizations to manage a collection of current and proposed projects. Using PPM, organizations analyze their portfolios to properly vet and sequence each project to optimally achieve strategic objectives.

There is no reason why PPM cannot be applied by individuals, particularly solo practitioners or small business owners. Given limited physical and financial resources, individuals can use PPM to focus on personal strategic objectives such as improving one's career, growing the business or penetrating a market.

By ensuring alignment of each project to the individual's strategic objectives, less time will be spent on trivial projects or ineffective activities. Define your strategic objectives for the next few years. Come up with vetting criteria for your projects. Assess all of your current and planned projects. Focus your efforts on the important projects and set aside the rest.

Tip 89: Suppress stress and ensure success by single-tasking

Despite the proliferation of mobile productivity tools, do you find yourself working fewer or more hours? How was your stress level lately?

Multitasking forces us to accomplish too little of too many tasks—which can lead to an inverse relationship in productivity and stress level. Instead of multitasking, focus your energy on one task and one endeavor at a time. Give it 100% of your attention and get it done.

Tiger Woods is a great golfer because he focuses on one sport—golf. You'll notice that even a computer will slow down if you have too many applications running at the same time. If you close all of them but one, that one application will run much faster. What made you think that you can do better?
Stop multitasking and start single-tasking to suppress stress and to ensure success.

Tip 90: Transforming teams in trouble

Herman Gonzalez told me that he has a great idea for a book concept. We brainstormed for 5-10 minutes and came up with the 3V Formation.

Think of the three Vs: vision, values and vibes. Teams get into trouble because there is no mission. No mission = no vision. No mission and vision = no core values from which the team's culture (vibes) can be built.

Think of the V formation: When the leader of the buffalo jumps, the rest follow. In contrast, a flock of geese saves energy by flying in V formation. More important, they take turns leading.

As a manager, your job should be not to manage time but to invest time in your teams. Mentor them to shape the three Vs and transform them from a herd of buffalo into a flock of geese.

—Adapted from a conversation with Herman Gonzalez

Tip 91: Select suppliers in seven simple steps

Sooner or later in your project management career, you will need to procure products or services for your projects. During the early stages of the procurement process, you may not have a clear picture of the requirements from which to base the vendor selection process.

Here are seven simple steps to follow in selecting suppliers for your projects.

1. Draft the business requirements documents (BRD)
2. Invite key vendors for initial meetings to get a sense of the various offerings
3. Prepare a selection matrix based on the BRD and the vendors' offerings
4. Ask the vendors to perform self-assessments using the vendor selection matrix
5. Invite short-listed vendors for in-depth discussions to vet their self-assessments
6. Address the discrepancies between your assessments and their self-assessments
7. Select the vendor based on the qualitative and quantitative merits of the assessments

Tip 92: Know when to report your project status as "Red"

Most people do not want to be the bearer of bad news. However, if your project is not really "Green" (on time, on budget, on scope, etc.) then report the status as "Yellow." If problems persist, say for a week, report the project status as "Red."

Some optimistic project managers hesitate to report problems because they believe that a quick resolution will arrive soon. In some cases, however, the problems have nothing to do with the project manager's abilities but instead indicate a lack of commitment of others.

Given this, it is very crucial to communicate the importance of the problematic areas to ensure the timely completion of the same. Highlight the dependencies and the potential impacts. Escalate the problems if necessary—but don't cry wolf. If you're still unsuccessful, then you'll have no choice but to report the problems.

Tip 93: Extract excellent estimates easily

Your manager probably has asked you come up with some estimates. Without well-defined requirements and comparable historical information, project managers often resort to randomly pulling numbers from thin air.

Such an approach is problematic because there is no good basis for the estimates. Often, the assumptions also are not documented. Moreover, you'll be held accountable for the poor estimates that you provided, and you'll have no way to defend yourself if questions arise.

To avoid this problem, clearly define the scope of the work that you need to estimate. Create a mini-WBS as appropriate. Look for comparable work from which you can derive educated estimates and make sure to document all of your assumptions!

Apply three-point estimating to address the uncertainties. Do not just blindly add contingencies—use standard deviations instead. Adjust the estimates as your assumptions become validated.

Tip 94: Schedule pre-booked meetings to ensure prompt project decisions

All alliteration aside, pre-booked meetings prompt prompt project decisions. Other than the usual pre-booked weekly project team meetings and the monthly project steering committee meetings, consider scheduling a recurring meeting to quickly address business, technical and vendor issues that may arise.

If you work with a handful individuals from various departments, particularly the decision makers, you know how difficult it is to book meetings that can accommodate everybody's schedule. It is usually better to have predefined times when the team can meet to raise questions, ask for decisions or discuss solutions.

If the meeting is not needed, it is easy enough to cancel. If the topic is not relevant to certain individuals, they can opt out of the meeting. By having short pre-booked time slots at least once weekly, you will have fewer headaches in trying to schedule meetings.

Tip 95: Impart the importance of project issue logs

As your project progresses, issues will arise from various areas—product, process, people, requirements, design, solution and so on. If not managed properly, such issues—and their corresponding resolutions—will reside in various e-mails, voicemails, hallway conversations and napkin notes. Important pieces of information might get lost or forgotten.

By creating a project issue log at the onset of the project, you can keep track of the issues—when they were raised, who raised them, what were the resolutions, etc.—and manage them accordingly. An expensive issue tracking system is usually not necessary; a simple spreadsheet often will do the trick. However, the former makes it easy to assign the issues, set priorities, send reminders and generate reports.

Go ahead and create an issue log for your project because if you don't, I'll have an issue with you.

Tip 96: Prevent pervasive pitfalls in project processes

Two extreme views of project management processes include lunatic and fanatic.

The former is foolish for running a project without any process. In contrast, the latter takes an uncompromising view to ensure adherence to defined processes. If left unchecked, both views can lead to failures or suboptimal performance.

Processes help you reach a particular objective or outcome in a defined and predictable manner. Although certain processes are very strict, wherein you need to precisely follow each step, many of them leave some discretion in the hands of the project manager.

Given this, it is imperative not to lose sight of the final project objective. Scale the processes accordingly, or if you decide to eliminate a step, document the rationale for doing so. If a process can make your project successful, then use it. If not, then reduce or eliminate it.

Tip 97: Master the art of managing virtual teams

Managing projects with team members in different locations can be a challenge. Cultural and language differences can make it even more challenging.

Here are some practical tips to manage your virtual team.

1. Meet face-to-face at least once, preferably at the beginning of the project
2. Share the calendar (project, personal, vacation and statutory holidays)
3. Create a common file repository and use the same software
4. Schedule a fixed weekly team meeting
5. Accommodate the various time zones when scheduling a meeting
6. Take advantage of the time zones (one team works, another team sleeps)
7. Leverage the technology (e.g., webcam, conference call, instant messaging)
8. Agree on a code of conduct (e.g., respond within 24 hours)
9. Be aware of the nuances of the English language
10. Have fun by organizing "virtual" social events (e.g., online bingo)

Tip 98: Manage bad news in your projects

Three components precede bad news: target, trigger and tweak. By recognizing these components, you can easily manage most of the bad news in your projects.

If the monthly expense target is $10K and expenses are trending toward $40K for the next three months, then the potential overrun is a trigger that should prompt you to tweak the situation. Inform the project stakeholders, but be careful not to cry wolf.

If you're able to steer the project toward a more favorable outcome, then you can report the good news. If not, then the bad news will not be a surprise to the parties involved.

Take a look at your current targets—budget, schedule or objective—and identity triggers that will give you adequate room to tweak the circumstances if needed. It is better to pre-empt than to be held in contempt.

Tip 99: Avoid major mistakes when managing project milestones

Project milestones allow us to signal the completion of deliverables or phases, or to mark major decision points. Unfortunately, project managers make two common mistakes when it comes to milestones: too frequent and too infrequent.

Although it is typical to have weekly or biweekly project milestones, these milestones are too frequent at the program and portfolio levels. Conversely, monthly or quarterly program and portfolio milestones might be viewed as too infrequent at the project level. A project with 46 milestones might look odd at the portfolio level if 4 to 5 milestones would have been sufficient!

To address these common mistakes, establish different milestones depending on the audience. When you present your milestones to your team, the weekly or biweekly milestones might suffice. For PMO updates, filter out the weekly or biweekly milestones and present only monthly or quarterly milestones.

Tip 100: Discover the secrets of getting others to help you

As a manager, I rely on the effort of others to complete my projects. I encounter the same situation on the board of directors and as a youth group leader.
My success depends on the willingness of others, some of whom are volunteers, to contribute small pieces to the big puzzle.

Over the years, I have learned the secret of getting others to help me. The secret is that I need to know exactly what I need before I summon someone for help.

"Can you please review my executive presentation for spelling mistakes?" is better than "Can you help me with my presentation?" "Please introduce me to a senior manager at XYZ Company this week" is easier to achieve than "Help me get a job." Others will be more inclined to say yes if your request is well-defined and time-constrained.

Tip 101: Learn to ask for help sooner

On my first consulting engagement, I spent one day trying to get a computer program to work. My manager noticed my frustrations and offered to help. It turned out that I was just missing a period! During my performance review, he suggested that I learn to ask for help sooner.

In scuba diving, if you lose track of your buddy, you are trained to look for no more than one minute. If unsuccessful, you need to ascend and reconnect at the surface.
At work, you should not be afraid to ask for help sooner. It is not a sign of weakness. If you are stuck on something, set a reasonable time limit. If you are still stuck at the end of that time, seek assistance. By spending one minute to ask for help, you may save yourself an entire day.

Tip 102: Make it easy for others to work with you

My old car needed a paint job on certain rusty spots. I'm hoping to get a few more years from it for my teenager. I stopped by the auto shop, got an estimate and then they took in my car.

I spoke briefly with my diving instructor to arrange for a weekend dive. I e-mailed her the next day, and she took care of everything. The common thread with these scenarios is obvious. Do you think I'll do business with them again? Absolutely!

In the office, make it easy for others to work with you. Reply to e-mails and voicemails quickly. Offer solutions instead of hesitations. If you disagree with something, honestly share the reasons for your disagreement. Life is far too short and precious to waste on petty politics and to be a pain in the posterior.

Tip 103: Familiarize yourself with the two reasons why others resist change

People have two innate traits that influence our daily actions: maximizing pleasure and minimizing pain. Certain individuals or groups resist change because of a perception, valid or not, that the future state might interrupt their contentment with the status quo.

Whenever you encounter resistance to change, identify the pleasure or pain states that people are trying to protect. If the root cause of the resistance is related to pleasure, highlight how the future state can make their lives easier or their work more enjoyable.

In contrast, if the primary reason is the fear of pain, communicate how the change can help eliminate or reduce their misery. Usually, dealing with one or the other will do trick. If you address both, then they'll crave more changes. If you want to win, pamper people with pleasure and ease their pain.

Tip 104: Harness the power of verbal Aikido

Given my martial arts training, I often find myself applying Aikido techniques, albeit verbally, when dealing with difficult project situations. Essentially, Aikido allows you to defend yourself without injuring the attacker by redirecting the force of the attack instead of facing it head-on.

In working with others, "attacks" are synonymous with dissatisfaction, insubordination and resistance because they prevent you from moving forward unhindered.

Dissatisfaction: I'm not happy with this project!
Response: What can WE do to make it right?

Insubordination: I have major concerns. I won't do it!
Response: How can WE address your concerns?

Resistance: I disagree with the approach!
Response: If you were to do it, what would be your approach?

You cannot face strong force with a similar force. Keep your cool and devise ways to transform the negative situation into a collaborative problem-solving occasion.

Tip 105: Prevent politics from pestering your projects

Proponents of the democratic system tout that it is the best form of government. Without proper checks and balances, however, the principle of "majority rules" (sadly, at as little as 50% + 1) can lead to "tyranny of the majority" toward the rights of the minority. Your projects may have comparable and ancillary political challenges.

Tyranny of the project sponsor: Listen to all stakeholders and keep the project sponsor abreast of various perspectives and their impacts on the project. You may impose, but others can always oppose.

Political red tape: Certain processes such as approvals and reviews take time; incorporate them into your schedule. Be optimistic yet realistic.

Community filibuster: Users may delay deliverables for pedantic reasons; be politically savvy. Deal with small pains for big gains.

At the end of the day, aim for completion and not perfection.

Tip 106: Learn to let go in order to grow

If you are still doing what you were doing three years ago, then you are not growing professionally. It is easy to grow as long as you are willing let to go.

A toddler lets go of crawling to get better at walking. A youth gets rid of training wheels to get better at bicycling. We sometimes switch jobs for a more challenging career. Yet, when it comes to our job roles, we tend to hang on to them longer than we should—especially if we like them.

As a project manager, it is imperative that you let go of some of your projects so that you can start managing programs. Replace 20% of your lower-end tasks or projects with more challenging programs. If you do that every year, you will soon find yourself managing programs and eventually portfolios.

Tip 107: Learn from marketers

Last weekend, I noticed a new subdivision sign that states "linked singles." It took me a while to figure it out, but essentially, it was a creative way of saying "duplex" or "semi-detached" homes.

I'm sure you have seen "pre-owned" or "pre-loved" vehicles. Yes, the terms are cheesy, but I admire the creativity of the marketers who came up with these concepts. As a project manager, you need to do a better job of marketing your projects.

Instead of simply rambling the project stats (budget, work months, etc.), focus your message on two items: revenue generation and/or expense reduction. If these items are not relevant, then highlight the emotional side with respect to the number of customers or people's lives that will be impacted by your projects. Don't hype the facts, but don't undersell your projects either; market them properly.

Tip 108: Express your interests and not your position

As project managers, we frequently negotiate with sponsors, staff, vendors and others. Instead of stating your negotiation position, consider expressing your interests instead to ensure a win-win outcome.

For example, if the project sponsor asks for an unreasonable deadline, don't say, "There is no way my project team can pull that off." By stating your negotiation position right away, you'll feel insulted if you end up accepting the unreasonable deadline later on. However, if you express your interests first, then both parties can continue to negotiate for a more reasonable agreement.

Offer that "I am interested in helping you deliver the project on that date. What can we do together to make it happen?" By doing so, the negotiation becomes amicable for both parties. You can then proceed to negotiate for scope adjustment or resource allocation to meet the deadline.

Tip 109: Watch what you say

On his first week on the job, a former colleague of mine was sent for orientation training. While having dinner at a local bar, two attractive women propositioned him. Because he was married, he politely declined.

After the incident, he excitedly recorded a voicemail message. Unfortunately, he accidentally sent it for global distribution. The next day, he received a personal message from the CEO.

The moral of the story is that you need to be very careful in all of your communications: e-mail, voicemail or even hallway conversations. You just don't know who will overhear or where your e-mail might be forwarded. No matter how excited or frustrated you are, think twice before you press the send button.

By the way, the CEO's message to my friend was this: "You are crazy. I would have accepted the offer."

Tip 110: Build your teams using these three no-cost activities

Tough economic times dictate that we cut costs. Here are three no-cost team-building activities that I learned from Scouting.

1. Ask the team to form a circle while holding a rope blindfolded. Challenge them to form a square. Remove the blindfolds to check if they were successful.

2. Lay out obstacles on the floor. Blindfold one team member. The entire team then shouts out commands to help the blindfolded team member navigate to another side.

3. With a soup can in the middle, lay a rope on the floor in the shape of a large circle. Give the team ropes that are longer than the diameter of the circle. Challenge them to get the can out without going inside the circle.

Debrief after each activity. Ask them to share what they learned about leadership, communication, teamwork and creativity.

Tip 111: Cut costs by blending team building and training

Just because your company is cutting costs does not mean that you should cut down on team-building and training activities as well. We could all use an occasional low-cost team-building activity to lift the team's spirits—and have the team polish their communication, persuasion and negotiation skills in the process.

Divide your team into groups and have them negotiate something— a mobile phone contract, flat screen television, letterhead printing and so on. Each group must negotiate for the same product personally and using only one other communication medium (e-mail only, phone only, Twitter only, online chat only, etc.). The first group to negotiate the lowest price wins.

Have each group come up with a strategy and then execute it. Schedule a debriefing session to capture what they have learned and which techniques can they use at work immediately.

Tip 112: Leverage three low-cost team-building ideas

A tough economic environment should not be used as an excuse to skimp on team-building activities. Times of negative news are the best times to lift the team's morale. Here are three low-cost team-building ideas that you can implement during lunch breaks.

1. Interesting Facts Treasure Hunt: Each team member submits an interesting personal fact to the activity leader. The activity leader lists all of the facts. Each team member selects 25% of the facts from the list and attempts to match them to individuals. Award prizes as appropriate.

2. Impersonation Video: Ask them to make a funny video of their manager. Watch the videos during lunch. Vote on the top videos anonymously.

3. Team Potluck Lunch: Have each team member bring a homemade dish to be shared with the entire team.

Tip 113: Brand your projects brilliantly

Give your project a brilliant brand—a name, an acronym or a codename that you, your stakeholders and future employers can easily recognize.

In the near term, the "project brand" will show up in all of your project management documentation, so make sure to use it consistently. In the long term, that same brand will end up on your resume. Choose a keyword-rich descriptive name—for resume bank searches—along with a memorable acronym or codename.

You are probably familiar with the Manhattan Project (a codename) but not the Central Artery/Tunnel Project (CA/T)—the infamous "Big Dig" (unofficial name) in Boston. Mortgage Web Sites Redesign Project is a far better name than XYZ Release 15 Project. Likewise, WXY Integrated System for the Enterprise (WISE) is more descriptive and catchy than Application Systems Standardization Project or The Power of One Project.

Tip 114: Learn basic accounting

Basic accounting is one of the key skills that project managers need to master to keep their projects within budget.

At a high level, you need to forecast your monthly, quarterly, yearly and overall project expenditures. Obviously, you need to compare your plans to actual numbers; this should be done at least monthly. Report any variations, and make the necessary adjustments as appropriate.

Depending on your project, you may also need to calculate costs for internal employees. Usually, it is a fixed monthly amount regardless of the position, which is then multiplied based on staff utilization. If you are using contractors, get their rates and do not forget to include taxes.

There are other expenses to consider as well, such as capital expenditures, fixed rate resources, hardware costs, software costs, equipment leases, one-time expenses, ongoing costs and R&D credits.

Tip 115: Avoid minor mistakes that even experienced managers make

In a recent project, I completed the schedule to redesign four mortgage Web sites for a financial institution. I was reminded (again) of the following "minor mistakes" within three weeks of my project.

1. Load your team leaders less than 100% because they need time to "lead" their teams
2. Leave some slack time for the initial tasks for ramp-up and learning curve
3. Schedule walkthroughs several days after the completion of the draft documents because reviewers need time to review before they can provide feedback
4. Incorporate holidays, vacations and other nonworking days into your project calendar before you communicate the dates to your project stakeholders
5. Send requests for access, permission, etc. early because they often require long lead times

We are all familiar with these common errors, but with time pressure, they're easy to make!

Tip 116: Improve your emotional quotient through self-management

Self-management is one of the constructs of Daniel Goleman's emotional intelligence*. It pertains to regulating your emotions and impulses based on changing circumstances.

At the beach last weekend, a mother screamed at her children and told them to go to the car for a 10-minute timeout. Had she regulated her emotions properly, she could have achieved the same results without creating a scene. It works the same way in the office.

If you disagree with someone in the office or someone really ticks you off, watch how you react to it. It is always better to understand the other person's perspective first before you calmly and eloquently present your side of the story. If it happens via e-mail, type a response immediately but DON'T send it. Go for a coffee, read your response again and adjust your message accordingly.

*Goleman credits Howard Gardner for some basic ideas on the topic of emotional intelligence.

Tip 117: Enhance your emotional quotient through self-awareness

Self-awareness is one of the constructs of Goleman's emotional intelligence. As a manager, you need to be aware of how your emotions can negatively affect your ability to build strong family relationships, gain the respect of your friends and manage projects effectively.

At home, do you do things that may annoy family members without you noticing it? Do you have an irritating habit that your friends might find offensive? Although you may be able to get away with your lack of self-awareness at home, it can be a career killer in the office.

Don't assume that everything is hunky-dory. Pay close attention next time. Always check your appearance, attitude and behavior. Are you aware of your nonverbal behaviors? Do you have a boisterous laugh? Do you speak clearly, or do you mumble? If in doubt, ask a trusted individual.

Tip 118: Temper the paradox of thinking outside the box

If you're like most people, your life is regulated by "boxes": a box alarm clock wakes you for your 9-to-5 routine. You leave your box house in your box car.

You get to your box-shaped office building and ride the box elevator to get to your cubicle. You stare at your box computer and then eat a square meal from your lunchbox. Your company boxes you in by telling you what you can and cannot do.

You check your mailbox when you get home. You get your frozen box dinner from a refrigerator box to nuke it in another box. To unwind, you watch a box or play some Xbox. You sleep in your box bed and repeat the insanity tomorrow.

For Pete's sake, even your coffee comes from StarBox! Creativity? Good luck!

Tip 119: Master the magic words to make your presentations better

Halina St. James suggested that you imagine prefacing your opening statement in any presentation with two magic words: "Hi, Mom!" If your mom can understand what follows, then your presentation is simple and clear. Otherwise, you will need to rewrite it. Consider the paragraphs below.

"Hi, Mom! We need to utilize proper project management techniques by adhering to the five process groups across all nine knowledge areas."

"Hi, Mom! On your next object-oriented programming project, think of the acronym PIE—polymorphism, inheritance and encapsulation."

"Hi, Mom! I would like to share with you the results of our project that leveraged the pervasiveness of social media to increase our revenue channels above industry average through inbound marketing."

If your mom responded by saying "Huh?," then you have a lot work to do to ensure that your audience can lucidly remember your message.

—Adapted from a presentation by Halina St. James

Tip 120: Don't forget that facts tell and stories sell

Whenever you make a presentation, you're essentially selling something—an idea, a viewpoint or a product. In your next presentation, weave a story with a vivid analogy around your data instead of simply stating facts.

It's more poignant to suggest "Imagine spending three-day weekends with your family every week" instead of stating "Our software will cut your processing time by 20%."

Or "California is the most populous U.S. state." Your message will be more memorable if you say "Visiting Disneyland, I came to realize that there are more Californians than there are Canadians."

Which of these messages will your audience remember? "California accounts for 13% of the $13.84 trillion U.S. GDP" or "I had a nice pizza for lunch, reminding me that if California were a separate country, its GDP would be comparable to that of Italy."

Tip 121: Praise publicly and reprimand privately

At a weekend camp, one of my leaders publicly reprimanded a youth for an unacceptable behavior. The same scenario could very well have played out in the office. In such situations, remember to praise publicly and reprimand privately.

If project team members did a great job, don't wait until the weekly meeting, the end of the project or the annual performance review to tell them. Praise them right away—in their cubicles, in the middle of a meeting or even in the hallway. Without embarrassing your staff, make sure that their colleagues can hear your praises.

In contrast, if you need to reprimand someone for unacceptable performance, make sure to do it privately—and quickly. Be honest and caring—and direct. Focus on the facts of the unacceptable performance and then ask for solutions on how resolve the issue.

Tip 122: Avoid the word that triggers people to raise their defenses

If a project team member performs a task incorrectly, don't try to fix the mistake by saying: "You SHOULD do it this way." or "You SHOULD have asked for help sooner."

The word "should" conveys a message of authority and superiority—that you know more than someone and are not afraid to tell him or her. Based on instinct, the other person will most likely raise defenses to justify actions or inactions. Moreover, you will likely lecture the other person on how to do things correctly instead of mentoring him or her on how to identify and avoid potential problems independently in the future.

"It looks like you had a rough time in completing that task within budget. What can we do differently next time?" By avoiding the word "should," the conversation focuses on collaborative problem solving.

Tip 123: Learn to manage your projects without the word "but"

Consider the two sentences below.

"You did a great job on that presentation BUT I didn't like the color that you used on the pie chart."

"You went through a lot of trouble to negotiate that contract BUT your effort was futile."

Instead of using the word "but," try using the word "and" instead— or don't use the word "but" at all. The word "but" negates the sentence that preceded it. Using the word "and" forces you to state the compound sentence in a positive way.

"You did a great job on that presentation AND the pie chart would have had a stronger impact if a different color was used to highlight the issues."

"You went through a lot of trouble to negotiate that contract. We'll use what we learned from it to close the deal next time. Good work!"

Tip 124: Manage your project's highest risk: you

Believe it or not, your project's highest risk is actually YOU, the project manager. Think about it.

If something happens to you, how will that impact your project? I'm not talking about fatalities but just the usual incidents that occur, such as short-term illness, temporary disability, family emergency and flu outbreak.

If you do not have a trusted backup who can run meetings on your behalf, then now is a good time to start mentoring that up-and-coming associate project manager or that eager project team leader. Give them opportunities to chair some of your meetings. Continue to coach them to take on additional project management responsibilities. They will be motivated by the challenge, you will minimize your risks and you will free up some of your time to take on bigger challenges. It's a win-win situation.

Tip 125: Avoid the wrong approach to weekly project meetings

Neal Whitten recently presented at PMI-SOC. It was good to be reminded of the correct purpose of weekly project meetings. You see, we all have weekly project meetings, but quite often we tend to use the wrong approach during those meetings.

Weekly project meetings should focus on anticipating potential problems, preparing corrective actions to prevent potential problems and getting a sense of the overall progress of the project.

Instead of starting your meetings by asking which tasks were completed and which ones were not, start by inquiring about potential problems that may come up next week, next month and so on. Based on that information, you can come up with corrective actions. After that, you can shift the focus to the third priority, that is, getting a sense of the overall progress of the project.

—Adapted from Neal Whitten

Tip 126: Don't dismiss options without considerations

If we don't keep our blinders in check, it is easy to dismiss options without proper consideration. As a manager, you need to keep all of your options open. At project meetings, watch out for the following pitfalls that can lead to poor decisions.

Ad hominem: in Latin, it means "argument against the man." Another person may attack the person who proposed the idea in order to discredit the merit of the idea.

Frozen evaluation: "We tried it five years ago and it did not work!" Unless all of the underlying factors five years ago are exactly the same as those of today, it is worthwhile to revisit the previous options.

Personal perspective: "I personally don't like that option; therefore, we should not pursue it." Incorporate the group's perspectives in addition to your own before making the final decision.

Tip 127: Manage multiple factors to deliver projects successfully

Project managers must manage multiple factors to deliver projects successfully. Here are some practical tactics for tough times.

1. Scope: separate needs from wants; focus on the needs
2. Time: defer non-essential deliverables to the "next" phase
3. Cost: check the estimates twice and stick to the budget
4. Quality: finish tasks correctly on the first try to avoid rework
5. Human resources: balance training costs with screw-up costs
6. Communications: reduce travel expenses by using videoconferencing
7. Risk: minimize or eliminate the probability and/or impact of risks
8. Procurement: always ask for discounts; add penalty clauses

With project stakeholders, mutually set expectations, relentlessly manage deviations and ruthlessly make the tough decisions.

Tip 128: Avoid the hidden danger of highly cohesive groups

"Groupthink is a type of thought exhibited by group members who try to minimize conflict and reach consensus without critically testing, analyzing, and evaluating ideas."

"Highly cohesive groups are much more likely to engage in groupthink, because their cohesiveness often correlates with unspoken understanding and the ability to work together with minimal explanations."

As a project manager, watch out for symptoms of groupthink in your projects: illusions of invulnerability, rationalizing warnings, unquestioned beliefs, stereotyping, direct pressure, self-censorship, illusions of unanimity and mindguards ("self-appointed members who shield the group from dissenting information"). If left unchecked, groupthink can lead to defective decision making.

To prevent groupthink, assign a critical evaluator, examine all alternatives and/or seek outside opinion. At the very least, one project team member should play the role of a devil's advocate.

—Quotations taken from http://en.wikipedia.org/wiki/Groupthink

Tip 129: Distinguish delegation from dumping

I received a message from one of my Twitter followers. He suggested that I learn how to effectively delegate tasks. He even had a matching URL along the lines of "Delegate what you hate to do."

Do you see a paradox here?

Delegation is not just about "getting stuff off your plate" so that you can do bigger and greater things. If done properly, delegation is an excellent management tool for succession planning, skills development and staff motivation. Getting rid of unpleasant tasks should not be the primary reason for delegation.

Proper delegation provides the persons or teams who will do the work with opportunities to try something different, perhaps even stretch their limits. If there is no challenge, growth and/or motivation that can be gained from the delegated task, chances are it is closer to dumping than to delegating.

Tip 130: Ask this quick question to qualify and quantify quality

In my consulting engagements, whether in Asia, North America or Europe, I often hear my clients demand high-quality results— appealing appearance, greater glory, impeccable implementation, minimal maintainability, rapid response and so on. The benchmark for the aforementioned high-quality results shapes the opinions of the stakeholders when judging, upon completion, if the project objective was met or not.

It is hard to measure "very reliable" or "user-friendly interface" or "well-documented features." Whenever you are faced with such "soft" or touchy-feely project success criteria, ask one quick question to qualify and quantify the quality expectations: "How are you going to measure _____?"

It is better for you and your customer to agree on "three seconds response time" vs. "it should be fast." Likewise, "within 5% of the budget" is far better than "may exceed the budget within reason."

Tip 131: Build the perfect team from imperfect people

Dr. Meredith Belbin identified nine clusters of behavior called team roles—"A tendency to behave, contribute and interrelate with others in a particular way."

We all have our strengths. Conversely, we also have our weaknesses. By being aware of the weaknesses that come with our strengths, we can minimize the effects of our weaknesses. After we have identified our ideal team roles, we can then recruit other project team members to complement our strengths and to keep our weaknesses in check. In doing so, we end up building a perfect project team from imperfect people.

For example, a good "resource investigator" excels at exploring opportunities but easily loses interest after the initial phase. A "shaper" thrives under pressure but may offend other team members to get the job done.

What are your ideal project team roles? You'd better find out.

—Adapted from http://belbin.com

Tip 132: Maintain a healthy psychological contract

In contrast to formal contracts, psychological contracts are informal agreements, based on mutual understandings and perceptions, between managers and subordinates. In simple terms, we can describe it as "You scratch my back and I'll scratch yours."

As a manager, you need to be very careful with what messages you convey to your staff—promises of a better project, higher salary, additional training and so on. Be honest with them, treat them with respect, set realistic expectations and appreciate their work.

If you deliver, you can expect higher levels of engagement, better results and trusting relationships. If not, the psychological contract easily can be broken. Your staff will be disengaged—doing "just enough" not to get fired. Once it is broken, good luck in getting the psychological contract repaired! When new opportunities arise, they will be gone in no time.

Tip 133: Know the one question managers should not ask

To get things done, we delegate tasks to others. We hope the delegated tasks are SMART—specific, measurable, attainable, realistic and timely.

When we want to know others' progress, we may ask, "What percentage complete are you with this task?" Given that question, we can expect the answer to be 80% or some other percentage. If you ask again later, the answer might be 91%, 93% and so on—but the progress may not reflect the correct proportion to the overall task.

It is better to start by asking, "How are you coming along with this task?" hen, ask follow-up questions to determine if the partially completed work was started on time and if the resources expended thus far are reasonably in proportion to the overall task, AND if you can expect the remaining work to be completed as planned.

Tip 134: Avoid the most common estimating mistake

Don't ask "How long will this task take?" because the customary response will be the "most likely" estimate, without considerations for the best-case and worst-case scenarios.

A staff member may pad a 2-day task to 2.5 days "just to be safe." His team leader may add a day for "good measure," with the manager "blindly" tacking on another 10-15% contingency. With this nonsense, the final estimate can easily become 100% more than the original!

It is better to ask for raw optimistic (O), most likely (M) and pessimistic (P) estimates—along with the assumptions. Manage the project based on the "weighted" expected (E) estimates with a contingency of ± 3 standard deviations (±3S). If the standard deviation is too wide, scrutinize the assumptions and revise the estimates.

$$E = (O + 4M + P)/6$$
$$S = (P - O)/6$$

Tip 135: Know these three terrific tricks to work wonders with WBS

The Work Breakdown Structure (WBS) defines the total scope of the project. The deliverables in the WBS will lead to realization of the project objectives. If you do this right, you'll be all right; do it wrong and your career won't be long.

1. Get pads of 3" × 3 " "sticky notes" of varying colors, preferably one color per team (or department).

2. Ask each team to write, in "verb-noun format," one task per note concerning what they need to do to help achieve the project objectives (e.g., "interview users").

3. Have the project team arrange the notes by work packages or by phases. Add tasks as needed. Finish by adding milestones, using the "noun–past tense verb format" (e.g., "interviews completed").

By using these tricks, you'll expedite team development—strong involvement and commitment—and also highlight the interdependencies.

Tip 136: Provide weekly progress updates

Project managers often use Dashboard Reports to provide weekly progress updates. Dashboard Reports typically list the work packages or phases in the WBS along with their corresponding statuses (RAG Status: Red, Amber or Green), e.g., "Package 1 is Green, Packages 2 is Yellow and Overall is Green." For the next reporting period, Package 2 might be reported as Red if the issues were not rectified properly.

Unfortunately, project sponsors "might be OK with Package 2 being Red" after they realize the complex dependencies across departments that contributed to the status being Red. The finger-pointing may continue without resolving the issues for weeks afterward.
To resolve such issues, list each team leader or department in the Dashboard Report and give each one a RAG Status. That shifts accountability to a team or a department instead of a "nameless" work package or phase.

Tip 137: Unlock the key to project success

You can use the SUCCESS acronym below to remember some of the key steps when initiating and planning a project.

- Select a dream (receive the project statement of work, business case and contract)
- Use your dream to set a goal (develop the project charter)
- Create a plan (develop the project management plan, collect the requirements, define the scope, etc.)

- Consider resources (estimate the activity resources, estimates the costs, plan the procurements, etc.)
- Enhance skills and abilities (plan for quality, develop the human resource plan, identify the risks, etc.)
- Spend time wisely (define the activities, sequence the activities, plan the communications, etc.)
- Start! Get organized and go (start executing the project)

"It is one of those acro-whatevers," said Pooh.

—From R. E. Allen and S. D. Allen,
Winnie-the-Pooh on Success *(New York: Penguin, 1997)*

Tip 138: Find the missing dimension in project qualitative risk analysis

Most project management standards advocate performing qualitative risk analysis to prioritize and subsequently address high-priority risks. Unfortunately, common risk assessments employ only probability and impact. These two dimensions, although widely advocated, are inadequate to analyze project risks qualitatively. What good is it to know the probability and impact of a risk if we have no clue regarding how easy (or difficult) it is to detect? To better perform qualitative risk analysis, we need to add a third dimension—the project's ability to detect a risk.

Based on historical records, we can determine the probability of a tornado or earthquake occurring during certain times of the year for specific locations. Likewise, we can determine its impact. But what if we don't have an early detection system? Our best probability analysis will not prevent us from getting blindsided.

Tip 139: Use the ACORN Test for project charters

An important component of the project charter is a measurable project objective. Use the ACORN Test to check if the project objective is well-defined.

Accomplishment: Focus on results instead of behaviors ("decrease complaints by 5%" is better than "increase customer satisfaction")

Control: Define a project objective that the team can control. The team can control project costs but not foreign exchange rates.

Objective: Ensure that the project will be considered a success if the project objective, by itself, was achieved. Otherwise, sub-objectives will need to be defined (not necessarily required to pass the O and R portions of the ACORN Test).

Reconciliation: Avoid conflicting with or duplicating the project objectives of other projects. Do not work in isolation. Check with other project managers.

Numbers: Quantify the project objective ("5% faster than the industry benchmark" is better than "improve system performance")

Tip 140: Learn to communicate with the younger generation

You may know ASAP, B2B, FAQ, IMHO and WBS. How about 10q, BTW, ROFL, TGIF and W8?

My younger sister, in her mid-20s, used to send text messages and e-mails using some of the abbreviations above. In contrast, I still subscribe to the old school of writing. When she started working for IBM, I told her to get her act together. Thankfully, she did. Now, we have Twitter!

As managers, leaders or parents, however, we need to effectively communicate with the younger generation every day. If we want to gain a better understanding of their world, we need to know some of their lingo—regardless of how much they debase proper English usage. By doing so, we can increase our effectiveness in managing, leading and guiding them in the right direction.

Check out *http://en.wiktionary.org/wiki/Appendix:Internet_slang* for more info.

Bonus Tips

Learn the fastest way to create a work breakdown structure (WBS)

Whisk through work breakdown structures by using WBS Chart Pro™

In the past, I created WBSs by brainstorming with my project team using a white board, sticky notes or projections of my notes using the old organizational hierarchy feature of Microsoft Office PowerPoint, a bullet list in Microsoft Office Word or the Gantt Chart view in Microsoft Office Project.

With WBS Chart Pro, you can visually create a WBS, as it should be, and then export the results into Microsoft Office Project. The bidirectional feature is really neat (changes in WBS Chart Pro are reflected in Microsoft Office Project in real time and vice versa). During your weekly progress meeting, you can use WBS Chart Pro to show a graphical summary of your project.

Go to Critical Tools to get more information and to download a trial version.

Make your contingency reserves 99.73% accurate

Use three-point estimates to make contingency reserves more accurate.

Duration and cost estimates can be greatly improved by incorporating uncertainty and risks. Unfortunately, some project managers simply pick an arbitrary percentage when allocating contingency reserves (e.g., 10% or 25% of the total duration or cost).

For each project activity, ask your team members to provide three estimates: most likely (t_M), optimistic (t_O) and pessimistic (t_P). You can do this for duration only, cost only or both. Use PERT analysis to calculate the expected value (t_E) using the formula $t_E = (t_O + 4t_M + t_P)/6$. Calculate the standard deviation (t_S) = $(t_P - t_O)/6$.

Manage your project based on t_E. Your contingency reserve should be +/− $3t_S$. Statistically, there is a 99.73% probability that the duration or cost will fall within t_E +/− $3t_S$.

Remember the most important thing to remember in a project

As Veronica Seeto advised in Tip 35, regardless of the size of your project, remember that you are managing people—not processes, not procedures, not the *PMBOK® Guide*! People will develop the project charter and the project management plan—and collect requirements, define the scope, create the WBS and so on. Given this, you need to take the time to know your project team members. Find out their likes and dislikes.

What type of work do they like to do? What motivates them? Do they need detailed instructions, or will a high-level description of the objective be sufficient? How did they perform on their last project? Most important, you need to treat them with respect.

If you take good care of the people in your project, they will take good care of your project.

Reaching your potential as a leader

"Leadership is scarce because few people are willing to go through the discomfort required to lead. This scarcity makes leadership valuable. If everyone tries to lead all the time, not much happens. It is discomfort that creates the leverage that makes leadership worthwhile.

In other words, if everyone could do it, they would, and it wouldn't be worth much.

It's uncomfortable to stand up in front of strangers.
It's uncomfortable to propose an idea that might fail.
It's uncomfortable to challenge the status quo.
It's uncomfortable to resist the urge to settle.

When you identify the discomfort, you've found the place where a leader is needed.
If you're not uncomfortable in your work as a leader, it's almost certain you're not reaching your potential as a leader."

—From Seth Godin,
Tribes: We Need You to Lead Us (New York: Penguin, 2008)

Tame the time tyrants using these three tricks

In his book *The Power of Less*, Leo Babauta advocated doing less to get more done. By applying three simple tricks from the book, you can tame the biggest time tyrants of our day—multitasking and e-mails.

Define your three most important tasks (MITs) each day. Do not do anything else until you have completed your MITs—no e-mails, no phone calls, no Twitter.

Even computers slow down when performing multiple tasks simultaneously. What makes you think that you can do a better job? Work on your MITs, and only your MITs, one task at a time.
Check your e-mails after your morning break and process it to empty. Do it, delete it, delegate it or delay it. For the latter, add the item to your to-do list so that you can remove it from your inbox. Do the same thing after your afternoon break.

Try it. It works!

About the Author

Dr. John A. Estrella, CMC, PMP, CBAP, CTFL, CSTE, specializes in helping senior management deliver large and complex IT projects. John worked on various consulting engagements for some of the world's most respected organizations in Asia, North America and Europe.

In addition to his management consulting career, he shares his unique and rare blend of expertise by authoring books and courses in project management, business analysis and software testing which are available in Canada, U.S., U.K., France, Sweden, Japan, India and other countries.

An eloquent and engaging speaker, he quickly connects with his audiences by presenting personal experiences, practical examples and simple recommendations.

John was awarded a scholarship by the Project Management Institute (PMI) Educational Foundation for his doctoral studies. He is a member of PMI, CMC-Canada, IIBA, CAPS, NSA and IFFPS.

On the personal side, he is a husband, father, Scout leader, martial artist, marathon runner, triathlete, scuba diver and avid outdoor person.

www.johnestrella.com

Notes

_____

_____

_____

_____

_____

_____

_____

_____

_____

_____

_____

_____

_____

_____

_____

_____